How To Manage Money

Assume Command Over Your Finances And Experience A
Lifetime Of Financial Security Without Anxiety

*(Effectively Manage Personal Finances Through The
Implementation Of Budgeting Techniques)*

Milenko Kirschner

TABLE OF CONTENT

Emergency Fund

As previously mentioned, establishing an Emergency Fund is one of the initial three measures you should undertake on your financial voyage. As we proceed to attend to and execute these straightforward measures, it is anticipated that we will promptly commence streamlining the more intricate procedures.

Suppose that you commence investing without adhering to this procedure. One experiences a sense of satisfaction when witnessing a substantial increase in their financial assets over a certain period of time.

However, you seem to have overlooked the fact that unforeseen events can occur. For instance, an individual may experience a termination of employment. In a similar vein, the employed party's spouse can also face the possibility of unemployment. It is possible that an individual's sibling may require financial assistance. A potential legal obligation may arise. An array of countless unforeseen events may occur. The corpus diminishes to zero.

Holding the belief that one is immune to such an occurrence is not indicative of carefree behavior, but rather displays a lack of wisdom. I express my earnest desire that such an occurrence does not befall you, although it remains a possibility for any individual.

No problem, you say. You will start again. However, during this procedure, one not only incurs financial losses but also misses out on harnessing the potential of compounding (additional evidence regarding this matter will be presented in subsequent chapters).

Assuming an arbitrary sum for the purpose of computation, let's consider an accumulation of Rs. 200,000 at the age of 30. However, it is essential that you allocate it for exigent circumstances. Had you possessed an allocated reserve for unforeseen circumstances, this amount of 200,000 INR would have accrued to an impressive sum of over 2,000,000 INR by the time you reach the age of 60, secured in a modest fixed deposit account earning an annual interest rate of 8%.

At present, high-yield investment vehicles are not even under consideration. Now, if you happen to possess the financial means to sustain such a loss, that would be excellent. Alternatively, it is advised not to neglect the establishment and growth of an Emergency Fund.

By forgoing the establishment of an emergency fund, you are not merely forfeiting Rupees 2 lakh in value. You are forging the opportunity for several years of compounded growth.

This represents a significantly greater detriment in terms of capital appreciation. It is within your means to generate additional income in order to restore the funds allocated for unforeseen circumstances. Unfortunately, compounding takes time.

There is no immediate requirement for you to have this fund readily available today, provided that you commence its formation.

One additional justification for maintaining a separate emergency fund in addition to your investments is that the majority of investment vehicles, such as Fixed Deposits and Mutual Funds, impose exit penalties in the event of early withdrawal. This signifies that upon withdrawal, you shall receive the principal amount along with the accrued interest, subject to the application of a penalty charge levied for the premature termination.

Avoid losses of time. It represents your utmost valuable resource, even in terms of investment and the process of compounding. Commence the establishment of an emergency fund at the present time.

What is the appropriate location for maintaining your emergency fund?

Credit cards have partially alleviated the necessity for maintaining an emergency fund. However, it is not advisable to depend on them. The occurrence of emergencies remains unpredictable. During that period, it is possible that you exceeded your credit limit.

Furthermore, the prospect of employing funds at a substantial interest rate is not something one would savor during a period of financial adversity.

The sole bank instrument that I would recommend in this book is likely short-term RDs. That as well, solely for this objective. Recurring Deposits are advantageous for the formation of an emergency fund, given that their locked-in nature serves to deter premature withdrawals. To provide further clarification, it is recommended to exclusively utilize this method for the purpose of building your emergency fund by making modest monthly investments. Once your portfolio matures, it is ideal to transfer it to a Liquid Debt Mutual Fund.

If you possess unwavering assurance in your ability to abstain from premature withdrawals, you may initiate the establishment of your Emergency Fund through a systematic investment plan in a Debt Fund itself.

Liquid Debt Mutual Funds serve as an ideal solution for the placement of one's emergency fund. We shall discuss these financial resources at a later stage within the context of this book. A fund manager, acting on your behalf, provides capital to companies or governments through loans and subsequently accrues interest.

Allow me to outline the outcome of depositing your Emergency Fund in the subsequent alternatives:

What is the recommended amount for this fund?

Consider it from this perspective. If an individual experiences a lack of income for a duration of 3 months, it would necessitate an accumulation of funds equivalent to 3 times their regular salary in order to cover their expenditures throughout that timeframe. Similarly, if they experience a six-month period without any income, they will require additional financial resources.

The quantum of the payment is contingent upon the unique circumstances of every individual. As an example, an individual residing in a leased dwelling will require additional resources. An individual with the ability to rely on their parents for financial assistance during emergencies will require a lesser amount of funds. The implementation of a cashless healthcare coverage plan will significantly diminish the required amount.

I would recommend maintaining a savings fund sufficient to cover expenses for a duration of 6-12 months, thus ensuring adequate financial protection in the event of unforeseen circumstances.

An Emergency Fund should not be misconstrued as the sum you habitually keep readily available in your personal possession. It represents the readily accessible capital at your disposal in the event of a potential need.

When venturing outdoors, it is recommended to carry an amount slightly exceeding your typical daily needs in your wallet. Do not burden yourself with possessions that could potentially cause regret if they were to be lost.

If you are at ease with utilizing digital payment methods such as debit or credit cards, mobile wallets, or UPI, it is advisable to maintain a modest sum of physical currency.

In addition, I would suggest retaining a single banknote of substantial value in a concealed compartment within your wallet or purse, to be utilized exclusively in circumstances where alternative means of payment are unavailable.

Comprehensive Examination Of Financial Statements: Uncover The Monetary Worth Of Assets, Liabilities, Networth, And Various Other Financial Indicators.

Balance Sheet

The Balance Sheet, also referred to as the "Statement of Financial Position," presents the monetary value of a company's assets, liabilities, and owner's equity on a specific date. Typically, this is compiled upon the conclusion of the fiscal year of the company. The company also compiles a profit and loss statement, which represents the aggregated expenditures and revenues over a specific fiscal year. The financial statement of a company comprises the Balance sheet, Profit and Loss Account, Cash/Fund Flow Statement, and the disclosures mandated by the companies Law Board.

The balance sheet comprises a concise overview of a company's assets and liabilities as of the conclusion of the fiscal year. In contradistinction, the Profit and Loss Account (Income and expenditure account) serves as a comprehensive report delineating the financial performance of the firm during the fiscal period that culminates with the Balance sheet date. The Fund Flow and Cash Flow statements are formulated based on the information presented in the balance sheet and Profit and Loss account. In order to initiate the examination of the financial state of the company, it is imperative to grasp the essence of these two aforementioned statements.

Definition of Financial Statement - A balance sheet

The balance sheet is defined by the American Institute of Certified Public Accounts as a comprehensive compilation of the balances in the assets, liabilities, and Net Worth accounts. It is essentially a reflection of the sources (origin) and applications (allocation) of funds. Alternatively, "From another perspective, the company's assets and liabilities." According to accountants, a balance sheet presents the origins of funds (liabilities and owner's equity) as well as the allocation of these funds into different types of assets and property rights.

3
Spend your Money Wisely!

Insufficient income is the cause of financial hardships for certain individuals. However, for numerous individuals, the root of the problem lies in their inadequate financial management or their tendency to spend beyond their means. Approximately 73% of the American population departs this life while in a state of indebtedness.

1. Monitor Your Budget

In order to initiate the acquisition of wiser spending habits, it is essential to have a thorough understanding of the destination of your financial resources. Establish a financial plan and diligently monitor your income and expenditures.

Once you possess knowledge regarding the destination of your financial resources, you can commence the search for opportunities to expend them in a more judicious manner.

2. Take into account the potential benefits and drawbacks in the long run of acquiring goods or services.

Frequent occurrences of impulsive purchases are a prominent issue. While this might be deemed acceptable in the context of purchasing a chocolate bar priced at $1 from a grocery store, it presents challenges when engaging in larger-scale transactions. Prior to making a purchase, it is advisable to deliberate on the potential long-term implications it may have on oneself.

What is the remaining duration of its existence? Would it result in an increment of your outstanding financial obligations? Does the cost justify the worth you will derive from it over its lifespan?

These inquiries can be utilized to ascertain the true value of a potential purchase.

3. Exercise prudence in employing your credit card solely for purchases within your monthly financial means.

There is no guarantee that your finances will be adversely impacted by the utilization of credit cards. In light of these considerations, it can be noted that they possess a practical nature, with many cards offering a reimbursement of funds on transactions.

Nevertheless, it is advisable to utilize your credit card solely for purchases that can be fully repaid by the conclusion of the month.

One will not incur interest charges as long as they settle their credit card debt in full on a monthly basis, rendering it virtually indistinguishable from making cash payments.

Nevertheless, failure to settle your balance in full on a monthly basis may result in a rapid inflation of accrued interest.

4. Cease your efforts to create an impression on others.

The average person tends to allocate an excessive amount of funds towards the maintenance of their appearance. A significant portion of our consumer purchases, ranging from high-end automobiles to haute couture, is often motivated by a desire to impress others rather than a genuine personal preference or affection for the products.

However, endeavoring to keep pace with the societal norms and standards can prove to be a costly and futile endeavor. Do not yield to the notion that it is necessary to expend funds in order to make a favorable impression on others; instead, procure the possessions that bring you pleasure.

5. Discern the Behaviors that Deplete Your Financial Resources

Once you begin monitoring your expenses, you may proceed to identify any habits that could potentially be causing you to exceed your budget. These behaviors may encompass extravagant leisure activities, regular dining outside, indulgent expenditure on clothing, or various other financial burdens.

Upon identifying the habits that consume a substantial portion of your revenue, you can then evaluate their true importance.

6. Establish a Appreciation for Saving Rather than Spending

Certain individuals possess an innate talent for financial prudence and derive satisfaction from augmenting their overall monetary value. Many individuals perceive money in a manner that dictates it should be promptly expended upon acquisition, viewing any other course of action as an opportunity foregone.

If you fall into the second category, endeavor to cultivate a mentality that places emphasis on savings rather than expenditures. Ultimately, allocating funds towards items with a limited lifespan or diminishing allure will invariably prove more detrimental to one's life than making financial investments or practicing saving.

7. Begin your investment journey at an early stage.

Exercising prudent financial management extends beyond mere abstention from frivolous spending; it encompasses the deployment of accumulated savings to acquire assets instrumental in attaining your fiscal goals. Given these circumstances, initiating or concluding an investment portfolio at an earlier stage or with a smaller amount holds no significance.

It is prudent to allocate your funds towards esteemed enterprises that exhibit potential for long-term growth, irrespective of your age, financial limitations, or investment capacity.

Foundational Principles Of Budgeting For Initial Guidance

It is an unequivocal truth that budgeting is not an easy task, which nobody can honestly deny. It is not until one has experienced multiple unsuccessful attempts that they begin to grasp the essence of things and establish a sense of stability. In even the most exceptional circumstances, it is exceedingly uncommon to encounter individuals who achieve accurate budgeting from the outset. During your phase of experimentation and learning, it is crucial to incorporate any available support and aid. Hence, the objective of this chapter is to assist you in effectively distributing your constrained income among the inexhaustible selection of financial obligations you possess, by adhering to a set of budgeting principles.

50-30-20 rule

Please take note that the mentioned income has been adjusted to account for taxes and contributions made towards a 401k plan.

The expression was originated by a pair consisting of a mother and daughter, who authored a book elucidating the concept of this particular approach to budget management. The fundamental principle dictates that an allocation of 50% of your net earnings, following taxation and 401 contributions, ought to be dedicated to essential expenditures or requirements.

One's necessities may align with your desires. Hence, it is imperative to adhere to your own perspective on your requirements, rather than being swayed by the opinion of your friend. Nevertheless, in essence, necessities typically consist of obligatory expenditures such as rent, utilities, transportation costs, alimony, and child support. These are expenses that necessitate payment, or else...; they comprise indispensable expenditures that you cannot afford to neglect. You are prohibited from tampering with this section of your budget, even in situations where financial calculations are incongruous, except as an absolute last option. This category encompasses mortgages, loans, grocery expenses, rent payments, credit card obligations, transportation costs, and so forth.

The 30% specified in the rule should be allocated exclusively for discretionary expenditures or personal preferences.

You may choose to abstain from incurring these expenses as they are voluntary in nature. Included within these expenditures are costs related to gym memberships, cable television and internet subscriptions, pet care, shopping expenses, personal grooming, phone plans, and charitable contributions, among others. You have the freedom to modify these should you desire. This denotes the net income after tax deductions, as well as the amount contributed to your 401k retirement account.

The final portion, comprising 20% of your income, is allocated towards your financial obligations such as savings and debt repayment. This portion can be utilized for various purposes including saving for a vacation, planning for retirement, or accumulating funds for a down payment on a property or vehicle. It additionally encompasses your contributions towards your emergency savings fund. It is advisable to strive towards maintaining a minimum of six months' worth of living expenses in your emergency savings fund. A portion of the identical percentage should also be allocated towards the settlement of outstanding debts and loans. In more straightforward terms, this section addresses your financial objectives.

Observation: It is evident from the aforementioned that there is no requirement to exhaustively allocate all the funds within each respective category. If one possesses the necessary determination, it is entirely feasible to effectively reduce expenditures across various categories. One advantageous aspect of this budgeting plan is its ability to prevent one from feeling excessively constrained by the budget through the allocation of up to 30% for discretionary expenditures towards personal preferences or desires.

The 80/20 Budgeting Rule

This rule represents a slight deviation from the 50-30-20 principle. Rather than distinguishing between needs and wants, the 80/20 approach combines them as the majority (80%) of all other expenses, while the remaining 20% represents the designated portion for savings or financial objectives.

There are disadvantages associated with this particular budgeting approach, particularly regarding its inability to differentiate between items of high importance and those that are less important. Consequently, one may potentially allocate funds toward less crucial matters prior to addressing pressing priorities, considering they are all placed within the same category. Nevertheless, this method remains the most suitable choice for budgeters who prefer not to meticulously monitor their expenditures. You may proceed to allocate the remainder of your budget after deducting 20% for savings.

Suggestion: It is not obligatory to limit the amount to 20% if you have the ability to set aside a greater portion. One could allocate 30% and expend 70% of their earnings. One may venture as far as they are willing, although it is crucial to bear in mind the significance of taking small steps, particularly if one possesses limited experience in the realm of fiscal management.

The Principle of Allocating 25% of One's Income Towards Budgeting

This budgeting principle endeavors to allocate four equal portions of your gross income towards all necessary and desired expenses over the duration corresponding to your income. Due to the fact that you are allocating funds based on the gross income rather than the net income, it becomes necessary to also account for tax planning. Allow me to explain the process in the following manner:

The initial 25% is allocated for the purpose of meeting tax obligations and covering other deductible quantities such as government-mandated contributions towards Social Security and healthcare expenses. The subsequent quarter of your earnings is allocated towards your housing expenditures, encompassing either rent disbursements or mortgage payments. According to financial experts, it is advised to refrain from exceeding 25% of your income on housing expenses, as this allocation may negatively impact other aspects of your life.

The remaining 25% consists of reserves allocated for the purpose of debt coverage and covering living expenses, respectively. One key distinction between this rule and the aforementioned initial rules pertains to the incorporation of the targeted savings amount alongside the living expenses, specifically allocating them to the final 25%. In this particular scenario, saving holds minimal significance as any minor shortfall can be offset by the allocated reserve funds. Pairing saving with debt repayment would be more advantageous as both clearing debts and saving are crucial financial objectives one should strive for, in order to attain a more content and secure future.

Excluding the inclusion of savings in the final 25% entails subsisting solely on 25% of your gross earnings, which may be manageable, but incorporating savings into that allocation could present challenges for certain individuals. If, however, you are able to accomplish it, proceed.

4-6-10-25-33

The aforementioned rule specifically pertains to individuals seeking to attain mediocrity. I have to add that it also has to be for those who are mathematically apt because of the involvement of many calculations. "I will adhere to the fundamental principles that dictate the allocation of your income as follows:

• One-fourth of the total income allocated towards housing, encompassing maintenance, rent, and related expenses. (26% or thereabout)

1/6 of the budget allocation will be allocated towards transportation expenses, including fuel, maintenance costs, and other related expenditures. (15%)

- 10% for expenses related to food, whether it is homemade or purchased from outside.

▢ A mere 4% of expenditure allocated to entertainment (1/25)

1 out of every 33 items purchased are clothes, which accounts for approximately 3% of the total.

I must express the truth that this particular budget does not align with my preferences, as I do not thrive when dealing with intricate numerical calculations, which is precisely what this entails. Another limitation is the absence of provisions for savings; however, this approach may be suitable for individuals who are newly embarking on their budgeting endeavors.

PLEASE BE ADVISED: There exist numerous alternative budgeting principles such as the 25/35/35 and the 30% guideline, among others, that will not be explored within the context of this guide. It is imperative to identify something that you can readily engage with in order to address the situation effectively. Pursuing something solely for the sake of it will not lead to a long-term journey that aligns with the essence of budgeting. Instead, it will result in exhaustion and hinder your progress at a time when you should be embarking on your endeavor. As previously mentioned, these guidelines should provide you with a solid foundation to commence your endeavors. However, once you attain a level of proficiency, you will be able to independently navigate and adhere to your preferred budgetary framework.

Recommendation: It is highly advisable to engage in extensive experimentation with a wide range of these budgeting principles until you discover a method that proves efficacious for your circumstances. Do not merely dismiss a budgeting principle based on its apparent complexity or oversimplification; it could potentially be instrumental in attaining financial independence by means of effective fiscal management.

As is evident from the aforementioned budgeting guidelines,

saving constitutes a fundamental element in the formulation of any rational budget. In the subsequent chapter, we will delve deeper into the concept of saving, elucidating its pivotal role within a budgetary framework, with the intention of instilling in you the determination to maximize your savings.

4. Generating wealth does not rely on chance.

Our aspiration is to acquire substantial affluence during our lifetime through means that do not hinge upon chance.

Many individuals believe that the act of accumulating wealth is dependent on chance or fortune. It's not. It pertains to transforming into an individual who attains wealth.

I prefer to believe that in the event of a complete loss of my financial resources, were I to be placed in any

English-speaking country without any prior knowledge or support, I have the potential to regain wealth within a span of 5 to 10 years. Due to the fact that I have diligently honed this skill set, I believe it is within the reach of every individual to cultivate.

In a grand total of 1,000 parallel universes, it is highly desirable to possess substantial wealth in 999 of them. It is not desirable to possess wealth in the small number of instances where luck played a significant role. We aim to eliminate the element of chance.

We are referring to four types of fortune in question.

1. Blind Luck:

The initial form of fortune, so to speak, could be described as fortuitous happenstance. I fortuitously experienced a serendipitous event that was entirely beyond my influence. That's fortune, that's fate.

2. Luck From Hustling:

Subsequently, there exists fortuity that arises as a result of perseverance, diligent effort, industriousness, and continuous action. This pertains to a scenario in which one engages in an active pursuit of creating numerous prospects, harnesses significant levels of energy, and undertakes several tasks, thereby causing a considerable amount of commotion and disruption.

It is akin to the amalgamation of substances within a petri dish, and observing the resulting combinations. Alternatively, "Or conducting experimentation by combining various reagents to observe their resultant combinations." You are exerting a sufficient amount of force, diligence, and vitality, which will attract favorable circumstances.

Mr. Nenad has diligently uploaded these exceptional videos on the internet, which I came across on the popular platform, YouTube. In this regard, he orchestrated his good fortune through the creation of videos, thus garnering the ongoing attention of individuals like myself.

3. Luck From Preparation:

Another method involves developing a high level of proficiency in recognizing instances of fortuity. If one possesses a high level of expertise in a particular domain, one will discern fortuitous occurrences within that domain. When it would go unnoticed by individuals who are not attuned to it. Therefore, one acquires an increased sensitivity to fortuity through the acquisition of expertise, knowledge, and diligent effort.

4. Fortune Arising from Your Distinctive Personality:

Subsequently, the ultimate type of fortune is the most peculiar and arduous in nature. However, that is the subject we wish to discuss. This is the space in which you cultivate an exceptional persona, an exceptional reputation, an exceptional mentality, wherein serendipity subsequently aligns itself with you.

As an illustration, consider the scenario where you possess unparalleled expertise in deep-sea underwater diving. You have garnered a reputation for undertaking deep-sea underwater dives that other individuals are unwilling to undertake.

Subsequently, through fortuitous circumstances, an individual discovers a submerged vessel containing invaluable treasure along the coastline. They can't get it. As fortune would have it, their good fortune has now bestowed upon you an opportunity, as they will inevitably seek your assistance in acquiring said treasure. You're going to get paid for it.

Now, that serves as an exceedingly exaggerated illustration. The individual who fortuitously stumbled upon the treasure chest was a result of pure chance. However, their approach to solicit your assistance in extracting it and subsequently allotting you a fifty percent share does not stem from mere luck.

You created your luck. You have positioned yourself strategically to leverage that stroke of luck. Alternatively, one could strive to cultivate fortunate circumstances when others have not actively created such opportunities for themselves. When discussing the concept of "without relying on luck," our intent is to endorse determinism, avoiding any reliance on chance or randomness.

In 999 out of 1,000 parallel universes, your desired state is to possess abundant wealth.

Allow us to further expand upon the concept that in a thousand parallel universes, there exists a desire for financial prosperity in no fewer than 999 of said universes. I believe certain individuals may perceive this and assert, "such a proposition appears implausible, as if it surpasses our expectations."

No, I believe it is not beyond the realm of possibility. Given your initial circumstances, I believe that you might need to exert additional effort in order to achieve your desired outcome. I initially emerged from humble circumstances, hence it can be inferred that anyone has the potential to succeed, similarly.

At present, I possessed all my appendages, my cognitive abilities were intact, and I had received a formal education. There exist certain prerequisites that are insurmountable. However, if you are perusing this literature, it is likely that you possess the necessary resources, namely a functional physical and cognitive capacity.

I have encountered numerous unfortunate circumstances throughout my journey. The initial modest sum of wealth that I acquired was promptly depleted due to my investments in the stock market. The subsequent modest fortune that I accrued, or more accurately, should have accrued, was negated due to the unscrupulous actions of my business associates. The third attempt has proven to be successful.

Furthermore, it has persevered through a gradual and consistent challenge. I have yet to achieve financial success through a single large sum in my lifetime. Over time, there has been a gradual accumulation of numerous minor issues. It primarily revolves around the systematic generation of wealth through the establishment of enterprises, fostering avenues for growth, and facilitating investment ventures. It has not been a significant isolated incident.

The accumulation of wealth occurs gradually, through the accumulation of individual increments rather than through a single instance.

The accumulation of my wealth has not been a result of a single exceptional financial year. It accumulates gradually, in small increments. Increased opportunities, expanded economic prospects, heightened potential for investments, and an expanded array of activities at my disposal.

Similarly to how an individual such as Mr. Nenad is cultivating his online presence and developing his personal brand. He's building videos. No individual's video will spontaneously bestow upon them a fortune in a short span of time. It will entail a lengthy existence dedicated to continual learning, extensive reading, and incessant creation, resulting in cumulative growth and advancement.

We are discussing the acquisition of wealth with the ultimate goal of attaining financial independence, thereby granting you the liberty to retire at your discretion. Not retiring in the traditional sense of discontinuing all activities. However, in the context that you are not obliged to be present at any location, you are not obligated to undertake any undesired tasks, you have the freedom to wake up and sleep at your discretion, and you are not bound by the authority of a superior. That's freedom.

We are discussing a sufficient level of affluence that enables one to attain liberation. In today's digital age, the Internet has considerably expanded the array of opportunities available. I am blessed with ample opportunities to generate income, however, my scarcity of time poses a constraint. I am currently presented with an overwhelming number of opportunities, and my primary constraint is the scarcity of time.

There are numerous avenues through which one can generate wealth, develop products, establish enterprises, foster opportunities, and consequently receive remuneration from society. The abundance of such possibilities is overwhelming for me.

What Do Currency And Assets Represent?

Currency serves as a highly practical \\\"instrument\\\" in facilitating the transaction of goods and services. Indeed, it is merely a prevailing practice that has evolved over time due to a multitude of factors.

Numerous individuals perceive wealth as synonymous with "possessing significant financial resources," often envisioning a substantial accumulation of funds resembling the wealth of Uncle Scrooge McDuck or an account balance of astronomical proportions.

However, wealthy individuals do not typically hold their wealth in the form of physical currency or in a standard checking account. The affluent individuals possess considerable wealth, a majority of which yields a reliable stream of revenue (despite the inherent uncertainty and unpredictability associated with the future). The assets that contribute to the wealth of affluent individuals encompass enterprises, properties, publicly traded equities, and others traded on the stock market.

Evidently, the affluent possess currency notes and current accounts; however, it is not their mere possession of money that has led to their wealth accumulation, preservation, and growth.

Throughout the course of history, currency has undergone significant transformations, with its manifestation extending beyond the conventional medium of banknotes and coins. The term "salary" can be traced back to the historical practice of using salt as a form of currency. The act of compensation did not entail the receipt of physical currency like notes and coins, but rather a specific quantity of salt, hence originating the term "sal-ary". Throughout various periods and across diverse nations, commodities such as rice, livestock, and valuable metals have also served as mediums of exchange.

Typically, precious metals were customarily fabricated into coins; however, their recognition as currency did not hinge upon the entity responsible for minting said coins, but rather on the quantity of metal present within them. A gold coin weighing 5 grams held equivalent value to an asymmetrical piece of gold weighing the same. The utilization of coins was a prevalent practice due to its facilitation of exchange; however, the intrinsic worth of these coins primarily derived from their composition.

A contrasting observation can be made regarding the present-day currency in circulation. These objects consist of paper and metal, possessing minimal intrinsic value. The value of these currency units derives from the authority of the entities responsible for their issuance, namely, the Central Banks.

The predominant means of acquiring monetary resources (or, to be more exact, affluence) are:

Currency denominations including banknotes and coins

☐☐ Checking Accounts

☐☐ Accounts with accrued interest and fixed-term deposits

Investment instruments with predetermined and reliable returns.

☐☐ Real Estate

☐☐ Listed shares

☐☐ Unlisted shares

☐☐ Own companies

☐☐ Art objects

The study of coins and stamps, known as numismatics and philately respectively.

☐☐☐ Collecting

☐☐☐ Precious metals

What is the status of investment funds and pension plans? Subsequently, we shall acquaint ourselves with the concepts of investment funds and pension plans.

2.1 The fluctuation of currency value over time: inflation and its impact on purchasing power

Hardly anyone considers money in terms of its purchasing power, yet the sole significant aspect of money lies in its purchasing power.

The amount of 1,000 euros can vary significantly, either representing a substantial sum or a modest one, contingent upon the purchasing power it possesses.

In 1970, a sum of 1,000 euros held considerable value, whereas in the year 2000, it assumed a more moderate stance. Fast forward to 2040, and its worth will dwindle to insignificance.

In our contemporary society, inflation tends to exhibit predominantly positive tendencies. This implies that there is a consistent annual increase in prices, leading to a gradual decrease in the value of currency. In the distant future, it is expected that prices will significantly inflate compared to the present, leading to a depreciation in the value of currency.

Is the amount of 1,500 euros greater than 1,000 euros?

Well, it depends.

If we are referring to the same timeframe, indeed, the amount of 1,500 euros exceeds the sum of 1,000 euros.

However, when considering distinct points in time, it becomes necessary to conduct a comprehensive analysis in order to determine whether 1,500 euros surpasses 1,000 euros or not.

Furthermore, this comprehensive examination entails assessing the purchasing power associated with those two figures at a specific point in time.

The fundamental question that holds the answer to this matter is:

What is the duration for which I can sustain my current lifestyle with the given amount of money?

The response to this inquiry will enable us to determine whether 1,500 euros surpasses 1,000 euros or not.

As an illustration, I'm interested in knowing the duration of time that I can sustain my current lifestyle with the sum of 1,000 euros. Suppose the answer equates to 37 days.

Now, let us fast forward by two decades and inquire, to what extent would I be able to sustain my current lifestyle with a sum of 1,500 euros per day? Let us consider the assumption that the answer amounts to a span of 12 days.

In the given illustration, the present value of 1,000 euros significantly surpasses the future value of 1,500 euros over a 20-year period.

Henceforth, it is advisable to consider money incessantly in terms of "the number of days I can sustain myself with these funds," rather than pertaining to specific currencies such as euros, dollars, pounds, yen, rubles, Swedish kronor, Polish zlotys, and others. From a rational standpoint, it is necessary to handle matters in euros (or the applicable currency), while internally it is imperative to carry out this systematic conversion into days.

Comprehending this concept is of utmost importance in grasping the true nature of money (wealth, to be precise) and gaining insight into its mechanisms of growth or decline.

Chapter 3

AN OVERVIEW OF BUDGETING

What is Budgeting?

The essence of budgeting lies in the creation of a financial plan. Exhibiting prudent budgeting practices involves ensuring that your expenditures do not exceed your income, all the while strategically crafting plans to achieve your long-term financial goals. The initial stage in cultivating financial literacy and subsequently attaining financial security and autonomy is the act of creating a budget.

A budget is defined as the official documentation outlining the strategic plans, objectives, and targets set by management, encompassing all aspects of operations within a specified timeframe. The budget serves as a mechanism for establishing objectives and offering guidance. Budgets provide a means of overseeing and regulating the immediate environment, aid in the effective management of financial aspects within the role and department, and serve as a preventive measure against potential problems. Budgets underscore the importance of thoroughly evaluating multiple options prior to reaching a conclusive determination.

A budget serves as a financial plan to effectively oversee future activities and anticipated outcomes. It is commonly expressed through numerical values denoting monetary figures, quantities, weights, durations, human resources, and similar metrics. In order to operate with effectiveness and efficiency, it is imperative. Efficient allocation of resources through budgeting is a strategic approach that results in structured and productive administration. Developing a budget facilitates the management of resources, enhances communication, and fosters motivation among staff members.

By means of implementing a financial plan, you possess the ability to designate funds in order to achieve desired outcomes. Any temporal range can be encompassed within a budget. It has the potential to be of short duration (typically one year or less), intermediate duration (around two to three years), or long duration (three years or beyond). Short-term budgets provide greater levels of specificity and clarity. The company's ongoing initiatives are evaluated within the framework of intermediate budgets, and appropriate programs are implemented to achieve long-term objectives. Short-term strategies can be derived from long-term plans given their inherent generality.

The duration of the budget period varies in accordance with the objectives,...

10 Advantages of Implementing Financial Budgeting

A budget is the most straightforward and efficient tool for managing finances. However, due to the supplementary exertion involved, such as tending to the lawn or addressing roof repairs, a majority of individuals opt to defer its completion. Creating a budget necessitates making sacrifices and abstaining from personal indulgence.

Practicing budgeting allows individuals to make informed decisions about their expenditures in accordance with financial limitations, exemplifying meticulous financial accountability. You will alleviate the strain brought about by extravagant expenditure and financial liabilities. Developing a financial plan guarantees the ability to savor desired experiences at one's discretion, rather than being constrained by fiscal limitations.

Despite the additional effort involved, crafting a budget yields a plethora of benefits that elevate one's quality of life.

Advantages of Implementing a Budget

1. Provides you with financial autonomy - Establishing a budget empowers you to effectively allocate and manage your financial resources. Budgeting is purported to enable individuals to exert influence over their financial matters, rather than succumbing to their overwhelming influence. By formulating

a budget, one can circumvent the anxiety that arises from having to suddenly accommodate a reduced financial allocation due to a lack of initial strategic expenditure planning. Furthermore, it assists in evaluating the merits of sacrificing immediate expenditures, such as daily coffee acquisitions, in exchange for enduring benefits, like embarking on a cruise or acquiring a new high-definition television.

2. Retain focus on your financial objectives - Refrain from indulging in superfluous expenditures on goods and services that do not align with your financial aspirations. Implementing a budget facilitates the management of scarce resources, thereby enabling individuals to navigate financial constraints more effectively.

3. Assists in comprehending your financial situation - By formulating a budget, you can gain a clear understanding of the amount of income you receive, the rate at which it is expended, and the destinations it is allocated towards. By formulating a budget, you can effectively mitigate the uncertainty of attributing the allocation of your finances at the culmination of each month. One can utilize a budget to ascertain affordability, capitalize on investment and purchasing prospects, and formulate a strategy for alleviating debt. Furthermore, it exposes your priorities based on your expenditure patterns, the extent to which it fulfills your needs, and the progress you make towards your financial goals.

4. Facilitates fiscal organization - Through the systematic arrangement of expenditure and savings, a budget

provides insight into the proportion of your total income allocated to various types of spending. If you proceed in that manner, you will be able to make alterations effortlessly. Your budget can serve as a reference point for effectively managing your financial information, invoices, and receipts. One can optimize efficiency and efforts by maintaining an organized record of all financial transactions, which proves valuable during tax season as well as when responding to inquiries from creditors.

5. Empowers individuals to proactively determine the allocation of their financial resources.

6. Facilitates the accumulation of funds for both anticipated and unforeseen financial obligations - Budgeting allows individuals to proactively allocate funds for unanticipated expenses.

7. Facilitates open dialogue regarding finances among your significant others - If you engage in financial sharing arrangements with your spouse, family members, or any other individuals, a budget can serve as a valuable tool aiding in the articulation and comprehension of your collective financial management strategies. Consequently, the occurrence of conflicts regarding the allocation of funds is sidestepped, fostering a collaborative environment towards attaining mutual financial objectives. Creating a financial plan with your partner will serve to mitigate conflicts and resolve disputes pertaining to expenditure management. Creating a financial plan instills a sense of fiscal responsibility within the household members, fostering accountability for their expenditures.

8. Provides an advantageous position in potential challenges - Through effective financial planning and the consideration of the overall situation, you can foresee prospective economic complications and proactively address them in advance.

9. Assists in assessing your capacity for borrowing and determining the appropriate amount - Acquiring debt can be a judicious decision when it is deemed necessary. Through the utilization of a financial plan, one can ascertain the feasibility of assuming a specific level of indebtedness or discern the maximum amount that can be assumed without experiencing undue strain.

10. Facilitates the generation of additional income - Through the utilization of a budgeting framework, one can identify and eliminate

superfluous expenditures such as late fees, fines, and interest charges. As time passes, these purportedly inconsequential savings have the potential to accumulate.

2. Present personal needs and financial goals.

Determine your financial goals, consider their significance, and assess the timeframe required for their achievement, taking into account both short-term and long-term objectives.

Ensure that you properly don your respiratory apparatus beforehand. Eliminating debt (especially high-interest debt) takes precedence over saving for a child's higher education.

Ensuring the stability of your retirement takes precedence over acquiring a replacement vehicle. A liability incurs financial expenses and can potentially impede your progress towards savings goals.

If you find yourself faced with a significant financial burden, the process of debt consolidation or renegotiation can serve as viable solutions to alleviate your predicament.

It is imperative to establish a contingency fund for rainy days. Only a mere 18% of residents in the United States indicated that they would have the ability to sustain themselves solely on their savings for a period of six months.

A suitable and widely accepted rule of thumb is to have a savings equivalent to 3-6 months of your salary in a high-yield savings account, and to further contribute to an investment portfolio such as Advancement.

Supplementing your income will expedite the attainment of your objectives. Not every individual possesses the stamina for additional employment, therefore, if you aspire to generate supplementary income on a monthly basis, it is advisable to request a salary increase.

Monetary transactions can often be intimidating, however, research indicates that individuals who partake in a collective endeavor tend to earn higher incomes compared to those who do not.

Indicate a Significant Quadrant

The book "Finishing Things" authored by David Allen has served as a crucial support system for Andrew, particularly in terms of directing his attention towards tasks and completing them.

In the book, David employs a quadrant framework to discern tasks that are urgent and significant. This is commonly referred to as the Eisenhower Network, and it can be described as follows.

You are likely to organize yourself in a way that minimizes the occurrence of significant or urgent matters, as they rarely bring any substantial benefit.

Another important guideline to follow is that tasks that can be completed within five minutes can be applied to various types of jobs. However, here are some specific financial examples.

■ Crucial: Mandated payments

Noteworthy: Pursuing an alternative employment opportunity due to personal dissatisfaction with one's current supervisor.

■ Of negligible urgency: Making contributions to your 401k that qualify for a business match is of utmost importance.

■ Insignificant: Let us now turn our attention to financial matters. There should not be anything present in this location. Certainly, perhaps we can consider incorporating the concept of master card stirring in this particular location.

Certain financial experts suggest the implementation of a personalized framework, such as utilizing post-it notes placed strategically on a wall. Develop an understanding of the reasons for undertaking the task of addressing pressing matters and strategize on effectively resolving and relocating them.

For example, the identification of automatic installment activity on your credit cards or the rectification of undisclosed transfers from your primary bank account.

If you encounter a dilemma or need assistance in choosing stocks or assets for your investments, consider seeking guidance from a Robo-advisor.

Do you require assistance in managing your cash effectively?

This document serves as our comprehensive guide for the purpose of planning equitably and effectively. We will guide you comprehensively on the optimal utilization of Mint, determining an appropriate budget, and effectively monitoring your expenditures in an automated manner.

Acquire supplementary funds within this fiscal year

Request a Raise

Seeking a salary increase can often prove challenging, particularly when lacking a sense of self-assurance.

Ensure that you are thoroughly prepared to present your case, and you will be pleasantly surprised by the extent to which your manager is receptive to enhancing your remuneration and elevating your status to align with your financial aspirations.

Furthermore, you will reap the additional advantage of fostering accelerated professional growth beyond your initial expectations.

Please find below a series of recommendations regarding compensation negotiation, which aim to assist you in effectively navigating the process of securing a salary increase from your superior:

■ Inquire about a resounding victory. Timing is basic. If you have recently concluded a significant deal, achieved a milestone, or discovered cost-saving measures for your company, take advantage of this opportunity to request a salary increase.

■ Engage in direct and open communication. It is not advisable to engage in this discussion via electronic communication such as email or text on a regular basis. I would like to kindly request a face-to-face meeting with both you and your supervisor and ensure that I have a sufficient amount of time to discuss the issue at hand.

■ Be ready. Examine several proposals that present a justification for why you are deserving of a salary increase. Prior to organizing the event, ensure open communication with your supervisor to engage in a discussion. I have compiled a comprehensive inventory of your accomplishments and, consequently, the value you bring to the organization.

■ Dress the part. However, given the relaxed dress policy in your workplace, it is advisable to opt for a more definitive clothing choice.

■ Be adaptable. Although it may not be feasible to consider a salary increase at this time, perhaps you can outline a plan with your supervisor regarding certain improvements you intend to implement over the next few months. During that time, perhaps a salary increase will be provided.

Address Financial Goals Sequentially

Focus on one significant undertaking at a time to allow yourself the chance to excel. If you attempt to confront everything head-on, you will become inundated. Making modest yet significant strides each day is the key.

Continuously update and assess your catalogue of objectives and track your advancement towards them, making adjustments as deemed appropriate. By allocating time and attentiveness to procure necessary items, you will be prepared to tackle more substantial and sophisticated objectives, such as engaging in land investment.

This is the ideal opportunity to generate substantial income and establish a stable financial future for yourself. It is imperative that you keep your long-term financial objectives at the forefront of your mind as you navigate through the aforementioned process.

Continuously engage in the study or documentation of matters pertaining to finance, endeavoring to amass wealth and attain financial prosperity.

Effective Strategies To Overcome Emotional Spending Permanently

So it appears that you have a concern regarding expenditures. Welcome, and I am pleased to inform you that you are now a member of our esteemed organization.

We have both bad news and good news to deliver.

Bad news first? If one is grappling with a challenge related to excessive expenditure, it is likely that they are seeking means to address an unfulfilled emotional void in their life.

It is insufficient to solely rely on finding additional strength of mind and persisting.

The good news? When we undertake the task of uncovering the underlying emotional issue, there is a reduction in expenditures. We have the ability to recover, utilize effective resources, cultivate positive patterns, and rely on the support of our community.

The Potential Disarray Caused by Emotional Expenditure

Emotional expenditure is a prevalent issue, although each individual encounters distinct challenges in this regard. Each individual possesses their own stimuli that result in excessive spending, distinct locations where this tendency becomes apparent.

In a broader context, it can be described as the act of acquiring items that are unnecessary due to feelings of ennui, tension, envy, remorse, self-doubt, apprehension, or any unfavorable emotional state.

That sounds simply miserable.

However, by dedicating time to thoroughly comprehend the origins of your emotions, you can devise a comprehensive strategy for effectively managing and addressing these emotions whenever they resurface, thus preventing their adverse impact in the long run. That is the objective I aim to assist you in attaining.

As the inability to exercise restraint over impulsive spending can lead to potential detractions from our larger aspirations and objectives, it becomes essential to consider the impact of seemingly insignifican purchases. And it instills within you a sense of guilt, stress, and remorse – a state of affairs that does not align with the kind of relationship you should have with wealth.

Tactics for Mitigating Impulsive Expenditure Driven by Emotions

Presented here are strategies that can aid in the mitigation of emotional and impulsive expenditure, while facilitating a shift away from recurring patterns of emotional purchasing.

1) Acquire an Understanding of the Distinction Between Expenditures on Mental and Emotional Well-being.

At first glance, expenditures related to mental and emotional health may appear virtually indistinguishable. However, in actuality, individuals are allocating their resources towards attempting to address an emotional void. The latter entails incurring expenses to avail oneself of additional assistance in managing one's well-being while grappling with conditions such as depression, anxiety, or other significant matters.

In broad terms, individuals grappling with depression and anxiety tend to allocate a greater amount of time than those who do not.

As an individual familiar with the challenges of managing depression and anxiety, when faced with sheer exhaustion and mental strain at the culmination of a demanding day, it is highly probable that I will opt for takeout rather than engaging in the task of cooking. There are occasions when I lack the motivation or energy to engage in cooking, resulting in my family having to rely on alternate meal options.

If you encounter comparable difficulties, I want to assure you that there is no reason for you to experience any sense of shame related to decisions of that nature.

I would strongly advise against refraining from investing in those forms of assistance, namely external meal delivery services, professional babysitting services, and professional house cleaning services. I desire for you to possess the opportunity to take those breaks at your convenience. Alternatively, my intention merely lies in assisting you in devising more effective strategies for managing those situations.

4. Abandon Outdated Practices - Overcome Unhealthy Financial Patterns

Inculcating sound financial habits in your children commences with your own exemplary conduct, necessitating the cultivation of commendable financial habits on your part. The actions you take hold an equivalent, if not greater, importance compared to the words you utter to your children. You truly aspire to exhibit prudent fiscal habits on a daily basis.

Here are some detrimental financial behaviors that you may inadvertently be imparting to your children: YOU LACK TRANSPARENT COMMUNICATION REGARDING FINANCES.

It is not necessary to delve into specific particulars, such as your income, but it is essential for children to acquire knowledge on how you manage your financial resources. Is it centered on attaining utmost pleasure, or does it also involve the prudent management of finances for unforeseen circumstances? In light of the fact that you and your life partner possess unique approaches to financial management, it is imperative that the two of you compromise and establish a mutually agreed-upon budget for specific expenses. In addition to inducing strain in a relationship, concealing expenses from one's spouse, such as the recent purchases of shoes or golf clubs, establishes an exceedingly negative precedent.

your kids.

You fail to accumulate any savings.

It is advisable to inform your children regarding your savings and its reasons. Urge

Encourage your children to cultivate the habit of saving from an early age. Though five years old may not be considered too young, you can achieve this by providing them with small amounts of money that they are required to save for short durations. For further motivation, you may agree to contribute an amount equal to their savings.

You display a lack of responsible usage when it comes to credit cards.

It is a common perception among contemporary children that currency is generated through the utilization of plastic cards stored within one's wallet. Elucidate the differentiation between a charge and a Mastercard, much like the comparison between the rewards you acquire and the interest you incur. It is highly advisable to employ cash as a means of payment for your children occasionally.

YOU DISPLAY INCONSISTENCY IN DECLINING REQUESTS: It is not uncommon to succumb to the appeals of distressed children at the point of sale.

Encourage them to leverage their personal funds or investment capital for their desired purchases.

You conflate desires with necessities.

Your offspring should come to the realization that they are unable to attain all their necessities in life. Each family's financial situation is distinct. Parents often feel compelled to provide their children with everything they themselves lacked during their own childhoods. However, this inclination often leads to a limited understanding on the part of the children regarding the true value of money.

You strive to surpass the achievements of fellow parents.

Children are not required to organize the most expensive birthday gathering, invest in an extravagant matric dance attire, or participate in costly extracurricular activities. Considering your financial plan, you have the option to present them with alternatives – would they prefer a bounce house or a clown? They must acknowledge the importance of life's aspects – it revolves around enjoying moments with their acquaintances, rather than obsessing over extravagant expenditures.

You do not possess the authority over your monthly financial allocation.

If you do not diligently manage your expenses on a monthly basis, you may find yourself indulging in extravagances at the beginning of the month, only to face insufficient funds thereafter.

To cater to essential needs, such as fulfilling financial obligations towards your children's scheduled educational excursion, towards the conclusion of the month. This type of expenditure illustration could potentially become ingrained in the lives of your children as they mature.

Achieving economic autonomy

You are restricted by the finite number of hours available to you each day and have a predetermined capacity for work. Thus, what is the rationale behind exerting significant effort in the pursuit of financial gain? "Attain the knowledge and skills necessary to generate wealth and establish authority over individuals, enabling you to allocate time towards more significant endeavors." - Robert Kiyosaki

I retain vivid recollections of my early childhood years, specifically an instance wherein I found myself compelled to arise at an early hour in order to embark on a journey. Upon the activation of the alarm clock, I promptly emerged from my drowsy state, brimming with enthusiasm akin to a lightning bolt, for the impending journey that awaited me. Embarking on a journey was a desire of mine, and during that moment, I would not have traded it for anything.

In the present day, between Monday and Friday, I am awakened by my alarm clock at 7 o'clock in the morning as a reminder that I must rise to commence my work duties. Currently, the way things are differs from the past; I no longer experience the same enthusiasm and eagerness to commence my workday. On the contrary, my thoughts upon awakening are occupied by anticipation for the day when I can embark on my retirement journey. While I do not harbor any aversion towards work, I would genuinely appreciate it if the employer were to contact me and grant me the opportunity to remain at home without any reduction in my salary. I would willingly exchange my employment with numerous alternatives.

Regardless of whether we are engaged in traveling, spending time with children, pursuing artistic endeavors such as painting or writing, or any other activity, it is an undeniable fact that we all possess personal hobbies and aspirations that we strive to achieve.

However, the primary hindrance in pursuing these passions usually stems from the scarcity of time, as we dedicate a significant portion of our waking hours to professional pursuits. An individual employed in a position that requires them to work from 9 AM to 6 PM experiences a considerable amount of fatigue upon returning home, lacking the necessary energy and inclination to engage in any extraneous activities. Consequently, they are only able to allocate their leisure time exclusively to pursuits they genuinely desire during the weekends.

Should we persist in the relentless pursuit of career advancement, our prospects will entail toiling until the age of nearly 70, rendering many of our desired activities unattainable at that stage. This represents the path of least resistance, the conventional route followed by individuals who perceive the existing system as the only viable option. However, an alternative path does exist.

The pursuit of financial independence is a challenging path, yet one that can grant us the freedom to engage in our true passions and interests. In the event that I desire to engage in employment, I shall possess the capability to do so. However, should I choose to dedicate a Tuesday to enjoying the outdoors with my children or embark on a two-week journey, I shall have the means to accomplish these objectives as well.

Attaining financial autonomy pertains to disentangling oneself from reliance on money for sustenance, and it is accomplished when the inflow of passive income (such as investments, dividends, rents, etc.) surpasses one's expenditures. We will explore the subject in greater detail later in the book, however, it is imperative to establish something from the outset.

Achieving financial independence is a challenging and arduous journey, but its ultimate rewards make it truly worthwhile.

It is essential to acknowledge that reaching the stage when passive income surpasses expenditure is a result of considerable time and effort. Therefore, it is imperative to have a thorough understanding of one's motivation in order to pursue this goal. My primary objective is to expedite the completion of my professional obligations in order to allocate more time towards pursuing personal interests. In my personal perspective, achieving financial independence translates to the attainment of early retirement, specifically an exceptionally early retirement.

The initial step entails discovering your motivation, as it is the driving force that provides the fortitude necessary for traversing the trajectory to its conclusion.

A large number of individuals partake in lottery games with the primary intention of securing their retirement or improving their quality of life. Attaining financial autonomy is akin to the aforementioned concept; however, it is characterized by a more gradual and secure approach. This methodology relies solely on steadfast commitment and diligent effort, rather than relying on unpredictable circumstances.

Time is money

The passage of time holds greater significance than material wealth. It is indeed possible to acquire additional wealth, but the invaluable resource of time cannot be expanded or replicated - Jim Rohn.

Individuals engage in the ongoing process of undertaking professional obligations on a daily and monthly basis, wherein they exchange their personal time in return for a remuneration which they subsequently utilize to acquire necessary or desired commodities.

The affluent individuals, possessing substantial financial resources to fulfill their desires, are not obligated to engage in employment. If they do choose to work, it is driven by personal preference rather than financial necessity. However, individuals who are not self-employed must diligently engage in employment to sustain their desired lifestyle and fulfill their financial obligations, including mortgage, vehicle, education for their children, and fitness expenses.

Ordinary individuals frequently possess financial obligations that necessitate them to exchange their time for monetary compensation, ensuring the ability to meet their monthly payments and avoid depleting their resources, commonly referred to as the cycle of repetitive tasks. When an individual purchases a residential property through a 30-year mortgage, their obligation extends beyond a mere financial debt to the bank, encompassing a commitment of three decades wherein their ability to cease working is contingent upon the absence of unexpected circumstances.

When engaging in a purchase involving a monetary value equivalent to $X, it may prove beneficial to shift our perspective from the mere currency amount and instead consider the investment of our time, as it is ultimately the resource we are exchanging in the transaction. Let us adopt the perspective that items carry a cost in terms of time, rather than solely monetary value, thereby encouraging us to maximize both our financial resources and our time. If presented with an offer to visit a destination with a cost of $30, and considering my earnings of $10 per hour worked, I evaluate the proposal as requiring an investment of 3 hours of labor before making a determination on attending.

The pathway towards attaining financial freedom entails the ability to allocate our time as we desire, liberated from the necessity of trading our time for a monthly remuneration. One can achieve this objective by generating passive income, which refers to income that is generated without the need for one's active time and effort. In order to accomplish this objective, we must initially exercise full control over our personal finances. We shall delve into this particular aspect in the subsequent chapter.

Choose Your Broker

What Is Risk Capital?

Risk capital, in rudimentary terms, refers to discretionary funds that are susceptible to potential loss. It represents liquid assets that can be readily converted to cash, in the event of any unforeseen circumstances or personal preferences. In the event of a complete loss, the financial repercussions would not be significantly detrimental. Risk capital refers to the designated funds allocated for speculative endeavors, typically employed in investments that entail significant levels of risk but also offer the potential for substantial rewards. The potential gains from speculative investments can be substantial, though the uncertainty surrounding the outcome of each individual investment should be acknowledged. Due to this circumstance, it is imperative that you engage in investment diversification. Not every form of capital can be classified as risk capital, nor should it be perceived as such. It represents only a fraction of your investment portfolio, designated for allocation towards private equity, hedge funds, or venture capital ventures. Nevertheless, it is crucial to bear in mind that every investment entails a certain level of risk. In order to attain financial prosperity, one must demonstrate a willingness to embrace this reality. However, when confronted with the appropriate occasion, one should not hesitate to seize the opportunity despite the potential risks involved.

Over the course of your lifetime, the volume of capital at risk in your possession will experience variations. Evidently, an individual of younger age may demonstrate a greater inclination to allocate a larger portion of their financial resources towards the category of "risk," given that they have a considerable number of years ahead to amass and accumulate additional funds. One might contend that an elderly individual, who has amassed a substantial amount of savings throughout their lifetime, ought not to put their nest egg at risk. However, given the presence of a substantial reserve fund, he would be able to allocate a portion of this amount towards venture capital. Notwithstanding, it is imperative for all of us to bear in mind the importance of diversifying risk factors in a manner akin to our approach to diversifying investments. Risk capital investments should consistently be offset by investments that offer greater stability. This significantly reduces the likelihood of complete loss. Each individual possesses distinctive levels of comfort when it pertains to risk. Hence, the most straightforward approach in determining the appropriate amount to allocate for risky investments is by evaluating one's risk aversion. If you possess a strong aversion to risk, it is advisable to allocate a lesser proportion of your financial portfolio towards risk capital.

Generally, it is advisable for the portion of your portfolio equity allocated to risk capital to not exceed 10%. An investor possessing extensive expertise and a distinguished reputation, commonly referred to as "sophisticated" or "accredited," may exhibit a heightened capacity for risk, enabling them to allocate 25% or more of their portfolio towards high-risk investments. Likewise, a trader with a substantial net worth possesses the ability to assume greater levels of risk.

Risk capital is commonly employed for speculative investments, including but not limited to private lending, private equity, day trading, penny stocks, futures, angel investing, options trading, and swing trading in stocks and commodities. Day trading is endowed with safety mechanisms that can effectively restrict a trader's level of risk exposure. As an illustration, let us consider the PDT (pattern day trading) rule, which establishes a requirement of at least $25,000 in equity for a day trading account. Neglecting to uphold this minimum requirement may lead to the suspension or imposition of restrictions on your account. Brokerages may also implement specific policies as precautionary measures; it is imperative to verify such policies.

What is Risk Tolerance?

If one's risk capital pertains to their capacity to endure substantial fluctuations in the value of their investments, risk tolerance pertains to their inclination to do so. Some of the determinants influencing a trader's risk tolerance encompass their accessible risk capital and net worth, which is calculated by subtracting liabilities from assets. When creating a comprehensive investment portfolio with a long-term perspective, it is essential to have a clear comprehension of your individual risk tolerance. It is important to note that risk tolerances vary among individuals and do not conform to a universal standard. What may be suitable for one trader may prove to be excessively aggressive or excessively conservative for your individual circumstances. Individuals who hold a preference for preserving their savings in a manner that minimizes risks often gravitate towards investment options such as certificates of deposit or bonds.

Furthermore, when making investment decisions, it is crucial for a trader to take into account not only their willingness and ability to assume risk, but also to integrate their investment objectives. Certain investments, such as those designated for your retirement savings or your children's educational expenses, are best positioned to minimize exposure to excessive risk. In a different vein, should you possess veritable discretionary funds, it may prove prudent to undertake endeavors aimed at augmenting your earnings. If a trader with insufficient capital chooses to undertake excessive risk, they may be compelled to exit prematurely.

position. In the event that the trader, possessing an identical amount of capital, chooses the limited risk approach instead, the process of recuperating from a loss will be swift.

In order to ascertain your risk tolerance, it is imperative to consider factors such as your level of experience, age, net worth, and available risk capital. Upon delineating these factors, deliberate upon the trade or investment that is being contemplated. Based on this data, you will have the opportunity to develop an investment strategy that is well-balanced and tailored to your specific requirements. Understanding your individual risk tolerance is the sole means by which you can ensure the alignment of your investments with said tolerance.

Pursue Lifelong Learning As An Enduring Objective

What Is Continuous Learning?

During your childhood, it is likely that you experienced a sense of tedium from the incessant questioning of what profession you aspired to pursue in adulthood, predominantly by individuals of older generations. However, despite the circumstances, you enthusiastically provided them with an answer, all the while contemplating potential new career prospects. In one instance, you might have expressed interest in pursuing a career in truck driving, whereas shortly thereafter, you developed a strong inclination towards the profession of a firefighter.

In the midst of adolescence, the identical inquiry regarding career aspirations was raised once again, albeit in a more grave and solemn manner. Your parents or educators expressed a keen curiosity regarding the career trajectory you would choose. Expressing a similar sentiment in a formal tone: "Merely expressing aspirations to become a truck driver or a fireman, without duly considering factors such as proficiency, remuneration, and expertise, ceased to be regarded as endearing." Ultimately, upon your completion of high school or college, your available choices had been redefined to encompass only one or perhaps two vocational trajectories, and this particular occupation or sector was anticipated to serve as your long-term professional pursuit.

Similar to many individuals in my age group, I succumbed to the misconception that my career prospects were constrained. Adhering to the false notion that my lack of previous study in a particular subject prohibited me from pursuing career opportunities within that domain. Due to my long-term commitment to a single career path, I opted for a stable and predictable occupation, resulting in limited opportunities for skill diversification and obtaining new knowledge. I had reached a point of stagnation and profound discontent, harboring the fear that I would eventually languish in the confines of my office cubicle, carrying out monotonous and uninspiring tasks.

The pivotal moment occurred when I engaged with literature focused on personal growth, resulting in the stimulation of my innate thirst for knowledge. I developed a profound interest in the intricate structures governing various aspects of society, the underlying purpose of labor, and determining a path for the remainder of my life. Furthermore, I was acquainted with the notion of lifelong learning which encompasses the steadfast pursuit of enhancing one's skills and expanding knowledge through ongoing education—a dedication that individuals are encouraged to embrace by seamlessly integrating learning into their daily routines to foster continuous personal and professional development.

The day you completed your education at college or university might have marked the final occasion on which you perused the pages of a book. One possible explanation for this could be rooted in the assumption that the acquisition of knowledge would primarily be limited to educational establishments. You might have also experienced the perception that, subsequent to attaining a qualification, you possessed sufficient knowledge and skills to confront a myriad of personal as well as professional obstacles.

Nevertheless, it must be acknowledged that education is not confined solely to the boundaries of educational institutions. There exist a multitude of alternative avenues through which one can acquire knowledge, surpassing the traditional means provided by textbooks or manuals. For instance, during one's adulthood, there exist opportunities to acquire fresh knowledge via:

daily interactions with people

Engaging in perusing educational newspapers and periodicals

following current affairs

online courses

mentorship and coaching

social media monitoring

listening to a podcast

supervising the operational effectiveness of diverse sectors

reading different book genres

participating in professional development events such as seminars, exhibitions, training workshops, and conferences

As a budding entrepreneur, the pursuit of knowledge becomes imperative in bolstering both one's business acumen and leadership capabilities. It necessitates a continuous exercise of quick thinking and discourages dependence on conventional approaches and regulations to address contemporary challenges. By persistently acquiring new skills and assimilating fresh knowledge, one can also ascertain methods to sustain competitiveness. You diligently remain abreast of the most current news and emerging developments within your specialized field, thereby enabling you to effectively acclimate to the dynamic and evolving landscape.

Effective Strategies for Sustained Educational Development

Being committed to learning throughout one's life is synonymous with possessing a deep thirst for knowledge. It is not imperative for the knowledge to be specifically derived from your respective industry. One may acquire information pertaining to diverse subjects, domains, or phenomena. A lifeline student is likewise committed to perpetually adjusting their methodology in problem-solving and discovering novel approaches to surmount obstacles. This cultivates adaptability and facilitates responsiveness to change.

The continued viability of your business hinges upon your willingness to acquire extensive knowledge and your agility in promptly adjusting to shifting market or economic conditions. As an illustration, your business plan may indeed be exceptional; however, due to a market shift, those strategies may progressively lose their relevance. What do you do? It would be highly advantageous to gain insight into the trajectory of the market and strategize a means of positioning one's business at the vanguard of this paradigm shift. Herein lie several efficacious habits that you can commence implementing within your business, enabling you to unceasingly acquire new knowledge:

1. Envelop Yourself With Individuals Possessing Profound Knowledge

Networking proves valuable not only in times of seeking assistance. In addition, your network also has the capability to facilitate the transfer of valuable skills and knowledge. In the context of a scientific study, an individual rat was introduced into a labyrinthine structure and presented with a cognitive challenge. An additional pair of rats were introduced into a separate maze, where they were presented with identical cognitive challenges. The rats that were collectively placed in the same maze demonstrated a more accelerated neural development compared to the rat that independently navigated the puzzle. This experiment substantiates the age-old axiom: The collective is stronger than the individual. If one is actively seeking knowledge, the optimal avenue for acquiring knowledge would be through one's personal network. Engage with industry professionals or convene meetings with entrepreneurs, engaging in dialogue, exchanging ideas, and sharing perspectives borne out of diverse professional backgrounds.

2. Develop the skill to discern and evaluate information effectively.
David Allen developed the Getting Things Done (GTD) task management system as a response to the challenge of effectively prioritizing important information when it is scattered

throughout one's mind (Scroggs, n.d.). While the pursuit of continuous learning involves absorbing a wealth of information, it is crucial to exercise discernment in determining what information is worth committing to memory. Inadvertently retaining inaccurate data or searching in incorrect locations can significantly impede your efficiency and focus. Allen employs a procedural approach in accomplishing tasks and maintaining focus by meticulously documenting all pertinent thoughts and ideas, be it in written or digital form, and subsequently delineating each one into actionable work-related assignments, complete with prescribed timelines. This process is commonly referred to as a 'mind sweep.' Engaging in a mind sweep can assist you in generating a comprehensive inventory of tasks that require immediate attention, pertinent information to bear in mind for future reference, or thoughts and ideas that can be disregarded.

3. Automate Your Learning

To ensure the assimilation of learning as an integral component of your lifestyle, it is imperative to incorporate it seamlessly into your daily regimen. What more effective approach exists to incorporate education into your daily regimen than to transfer it onto your cellular device or personal computer? Automation leverages data and computational algorithms to facilitate the filtration of information, enabling the curation of personalized news feeds that exclusively display content sourced from preferred websites and other reputable sources. This feature offers significant time-saving benefits as your computer takes charge of the process of selecting and organizing information, relieving you of the need to do so manually. Data aggregation software, such as Trifacta, possesses the capability to facilitate the consolidation of information from various sources into a central repository, thereby simplifying tasks such as data filtering, analysis, and reporting.

4. Learn in Small Intervals

Rather than attempting to condense a large amount of information into one session, your ability to comprehend and retain information is enhanced when you space out your learning. One may allocate specific time intervals every day to engage in activities such as delving into a particular subject, perusing literature, or keeping abreast of current events. Throughout this period, it is advisable to engage in the habit of incorporating brief intervals of silence, thus allowing oneself the opportunity to contemplate and assimilate the information one has gained from reading or listening, prior to progressing further.

Should the recently acquired information stimulate a notion or consideration, take a pause and proceed to pursue your line of contemplation. One may choose to allocate a brief moment to record notable keywords, themes, or ideas that warrant more profound examination at a later juncture.

5. Reflect on Your Learning

Following the acquisition of new knowledge, it is prudent to allocate a period of time for the purpose of summarizing the newfound information and its potential implications on both personal and professional domains. For instance, in the event that you receive a broadcast communication indicating an increase in the cost of fuel, contemplate how such information may potentially impact various aspects of your professional pursuits, domestic routines, personal well-being, and the like.

Develop the practice of evaluating the importance of your acquired knowledge, as it is often within ordinary life situations that remarkable business innovations can be discovered. Additionally, you may engage in introspection regarding your learning by seeking out an individual with whom you can impart your knowledge. Discoursing upon acquired knowledge constitutes a mode of reiteration, affording an additional chance to assimilate and retain information within the recesses of one's long-term memory.

What are the necessary prerequisites for a successful credit card application?

In order to proceed with your application, it is a prerequisite that you have attained the age of at least 18 years.

It is essential that you possess gainful employment and have fulfilled the mandatory probationary period stipulated by your employer, typically within a duration of 3 to 6 months.

Kindly ensure the fulfillment of the credit card application form provided by your preferred bank, and proceed to submit all pertinent supporting documentation as per their stipulations relevant to your circumstances.

Please expect a response from the financial institution or bank within a period of approximately 7 to 14 days. If you do not receive a response within this timeframe, you are welcome to contact the company directly and request to be connected to the department responsible for credit card inquiries.

Kindly inquire about the status of your application, with the hope that by the conclusion of our conversation, you will have received approval.

In the event that your application is not approved, the banks, through their internal evaluation process, have determined that you either possess a higher level of risk or lack the required financial stability necessary for them to grant you a credit card at this juncture.

Suppose you are currently not granted approval; this denotes that you may continue with your work endeavors and establish stability before reapplying after a period of six months.

The Prevailing Fallacies Surrounding Credit Card Ownership"; or "The

Misunderstandings and False Beliefs Regarding Credit Card Ownership

You do not possess significant wealth, therefore it is advisable to refrain from creating an impression of affluence and ostentatiously displaying it.

A credit card does not constitute an asset, rather it represents a liability, albeit a conspicuous one.

Do not disburse your cash assets in anticipation of relying on your credit card for sustenance until the borrowed funds are fully reimbursed.

Exercise control over your financial constraints and restrict your expenditures to an amount that can be comfortably reimbursed within a period of one (1) to two (2) months.

In the event that a credit card is declined, it is important to maintain composure as such occurrences can happen to any individual.

In the event that you do not receive a statement for your credit card this month, it implies that you are not obligated to remit the minimum payment by the designated deadline. It is solely your responsibility to maintain awareness of your credit card balance and ensure timely payment.

If you are experiencing financial constraints, I would recommend refraining from making a payment to the bank this month. The imposition of late charges, fees for exceeding credit limits, and miscellaneous service charges do not justify the associated costs. It is advisable to settle your credit card payment early in the month rather than experiencing financial constraints when the due date arrives. The bank imposes no limitations on payment at any point throughout the month. One must simply be aware of their "statement date" and proceed to submit the payment subsequent to said date.

Assortment of Credit Card Options"
"Varieties of Credit Cards Offered"
"Diverse Range of Credit Card Choices"
"Various Credit Card Selections

The three (3) most popular and renowned types are;
- The financial institution known as American Express
Visa card
Regarding the payment card, MasterCard

Each of these also exists in various forms, as demonstrated by the following examples;

- Classic

- Gold bullion - Precious metal with a yellow luster - Valuable commodity with a metallic hue - Noble element possessing a shimmering appearance - Highly regarded material with a radiant sheen

- Aero Platinum or the Platinum variant

- Card in the color black

Please take note. The primary distinctions lie in the "card limits" and the required income bracket for qualification in each of these cases.

Varied credit card offerings tailored to specific needs such as cash back rewards on categories including gas, travel, grocery, and general cash back are available based on the geographical location of residence. to cater to the diverse requirements of their clientele. It is imperative to carefully peruse and conduct thorough research to determine the most appropriate and practical card option for your needs. Although you meet the requirements for a "Gold Card," it may not necessarily be advantageous to apply for it. Perhaps it would be more suitable for you to consider applying for the Classic Card with its lower limit. This is the juncture at which you must engage in candid self-reflection and evaluate your capacity to exercise fiscal control within the confines of your expenditure parameters. Take a moment to reflect upon whether you possess the capacity to refrain from acquiring unnecessary items or if you are inclined to adopt the behavior of an Eskimo procuring ice.

Tips For Success: A Guide To Effective Money Management

Although money cannot procure happiness, it can engender a sense of security if one exercises prudent financial management. Lacking knowledge in the field of financial management, one might consistently experience a sense of precariousness, as if their life is constantly on the verge of a fiscal precipice. Moreover, you would certainly lack any inclination to venture near the edge of the abyss, would you not?

Indeed, it is a factual reality that a quarter of the American population express a continual state of anxiety regarding their financial circumstances. Moreover, studies have revealed that a notable majority of 37% of Americans would resort to employing a credit card in order to address a monetary crisis amounting to $1,000. It is imperative that you make a concerted effort to refrain from such behavior in situations of this nature, as doing so necessitates a thorough understanding of financial management.

When one effectively manages their finances, life may not become simpler, yet it grants them additional freedom to concentrate on vital aspects of their existence. Fortunately, the process of aligning your finances can be easily accomplished. We should delve into the proper manner of managing your finances.

19 Strategies for prudent financial management

Managing your finances does not need to be overwhelming. Prudently implement these financial management strategies sequentially to gain control over your economic resources.

1. Establish the appropriate financial records

Appropriate financial accounts are fundamental to the attainment of your financial success because attempting to manage your finances without the appropriate banking relationships is akin to attempting to maintain your vehicle without the necessary components. You will be required to establish checking, savings, and investment accounts.

These components are the fundamental building blocks of financial success. It is imperative to establish both a checking and investment account in order to easily distinguish between expendable funds and long-term savings. Leaving your reserve funds solely within your financial records renders them susceptible to inadvertent depletion, thus increasing the chances of unintentional expenditure.

2. Please review your current financial situation.

In spite of its potential intimidation, progress in one's financial situation cannot be achieved without acknowledging the ongoing circumstances. It is imperative for you to impartially assess any lingering commitments or substantial expenses that are adversely impacting your financial plan.

Commend your excellent financial choices. Take note of all occurrences with the intention of being able to fully appreciate the circumstances.

3. Establish a strategic financial framework.

In the absence of proper financial planning, individuals might easily find themselves in a precarious financial situation due to the heightened tendency to exceed their budget. Taking everything into account, the notion of indulging oneself is alluring to adopt. If you agree to incur excessive and unnecessary expenses, you may find yourself dissatisfied with the state of your savings. To combat this issue, allocate a certain amount of surplus to establish a comprehensive budget.

Devise a strategic allocation plan for your financial resources. In light of your usual expenditures, I urge you to contemplate your financial goals in anticipation of the future. Similarly, it is imperative for you to discover an effective financial planning strategy that will facilitate the management of your funds.

4. Establish appropriate financial objectives.

If you are seeking to engage in responsible handling of your finances, setting financial objectives is a fundamental principle of effective money management. Establishing clear financial goals will serve as a guiding framework, ensuring your financial path remains on course and motivating you towards achieving your desired financial outcomes.

There is no incorrect or misguided response; however, it is necessary for you to take a moment to contemplate your plans and consider the financial aspect associated with them. When contemplating the role of money in your life, establish clear and specific objectives for your financial resources.

5. Ensure a daily review of your financial standing.

One cannot make progress without being aware of their current position, as this lack of awareness would hinder them from determining their starting point. Kindly allocate five minutes on a regular basis to review your financial plan. Is it plausible to assert that you are engaging in excessive expenditure? Could it be posited that you are in an aesthetically pleasing state? It is crucial to have this knowledge as it enables you to make necessary modifications.

It may appear tedious to continuously examine your financial situation. In any event, it does not necessarily necessitate a substantial time commitment. Employ a software application or financial spreadsheet to expeditiously assess your financial status and resume your regular activities.

Implementing computerization for managing your finances can effectively contribute to simplifying your daily life.

6. Reduce your expenditures

As you commence a more careful examination of your finances, it is advisable to first scrutinize your expenditures. Investigate potential areas where expenses can be eliminated from your monthly budget. In any case, eliminating an insignificant expenditure of merely $10 from your budget can lead to savings of $120 annually.

Candid suggestions for items to eliminate could include office snacks, a subscription service, or your internet package. Reducing your expenditure strategy is an exemplary method of financial management that can greatly facilitate the process of saving.

7. Investigate your income

While it may seem remarkably obvious, it is crucial to ascertain the precise nature of the item you acquire. Please take a moment to calculate your total income after deductions and taxes, as well as your net salary. You will enhance your financial planning abilities by utilizing this precise figure.

If you find yourself feeling discouraged by your current total income, it may be prudent to consider pursuing supplementary employment opportunities. A lucrative remote part-time opportunity can seamlessly fit into your schedule and contribute to the positive growth of your finances.

An additional strategy for bolstering your income is to negotiate your salary. You are encouraged to approach your supervisor with relevant information that supports your request for a salary increase. It is difficult to determine the potential contributions that individuals may possess.

Chapter 3

The 3 Ds

Transitioning from a state of desire to the stage of implementation can pose a considerable challenge. Although the act itself may appear straightforward, numerous individuals often struggle to bridge the gap between aspiration and action due to a lack of proficiency in certain areas. Mastering the three qualities of decision-making, discipline, and determination is an exemplary approach to reaching the stage of taking action.

Decision

What is the definition of decision-making? In my perspective, that implies arriving at a conclusive determination in order to accomplish an objective or engage in an activity. Nevertheless, for a considerable number of individuals, reaching a decision does not carry excessive gravity. It is another remark that you make. It is of utmost significance that one approaches the task of managing their finances or acquiring the requisite habits with earnestness, refraining from any semblance of mediocrity.

I lacked proficiency in decision-making, which consequently caused me to expend substantial amounts of time deliberating and wavering between my objectives. However, the realization that dawned upon me was as follows. Upon firmly reaching a definitive determination regarding your aspirations and the strategies to be employed in their realization, you will find that attaining your goals becomes markedly easier, thereby eliminating the need to incessantly ponder the feasibility of your chosen path. The ability to decisively make choices will significantly impact the efficiency and effectiveness with which you establish these new habits. In order to facilitate decision-making, it is advantageous to acquire a solid education on the subject matter of interest, along with discerning the precise motivation for undertaking such a pursuit.

Discipline

The extent of your discipline will largely dictate the degree of your consistency. In addition to your desire to assume responsibility for your finances, you also wish to exercise self-discipline in your decision-making.

Throughout my childhood, whenever my actions deviated from the expected norms, my father would admonish me by stating, "You lack discipline." At that time, I failed to grasp the underlying meaning behind his words, as I perceived them as nonsensical. Upon reflection, it becomes evident that his words held considerable validity. He astutely observed our lack of self-discipline, as our behavior demonstrated sporadic adherence to what was morally right, while predominantly succumbing to our inability to exercise control over our actions. In regards to cultivating habits, discipline is vital as it enables individuals to consistently engage in repetitive actions and thoughts, thereby facilitating the permanent integration of these behaviors within oneself. Similar to the melody that you hold dear, the lyrics remain etched in your memory despite the passage of time. Also, refusing to relinquish that vice, alongside routine activities such as walking, eating, or driving, exemplify your unwavering commitment. It is worth noting that the formation of a habit typically requires a period of 21 days.

An effective strategy for maintaining discipline involves identifying methods to derive pleasure from one's tasks. If one derives pleasure from his or her activities, there will be no hindrance in performing them consistently or repetitively.

Determination

To what extent are you prepared to proceed? Managing your finances will not be a one-off occurrence, nor will it be a short-term endeavor but rather a long-term commitment. There may be instances where maintaining composure becomes challenging. Initially, individuals may assert that the endeavor is ineffectual, and even your own inner voice may convey the same belief. I would like to inquire whether, during those aforementioned periods, you will possess the fortitude necessary to persevere and overcome the challenges that lie ahead, ultimately emerging into a more favorable and optimistic state.

I previously alluded to the fact that it required a span of several months for me to acclimate to the rhythm and demands of the situation. During those months, I was frequently oscillating between my commitments, experiencing moments when I strongly contemplated abandoning everything and discontinuing my pursuits entirely. However, I refrained from doing so due to the presence of a compelling motive. My aspiration to improve my financial situation, coupled with the realization that others had achieved similar results, led me to believe that I could perhaps excel in this endeavor.

The most valuable counsel, if one desires to uphold unwavering commitment to their monetary management aspirations, is to cultivate a robust sense of purpose or underlying motive. The rationale behind your imperative to not only want, but to also necessitate the success of this endeavor. It will prove instrumental in enabling you to persevere amidst adversity and doubt that may arise. And please bear in mind that attaining perfection is not a prerequisite for achieving success; you need only maintain a steadfast determination to persevere.

Getting a Job

This section does not pertain to effective methods of writing your resume or conducting a successful interview. There is an abundance of educational literature available to aid in that endeavor. This configuration of equipment is intended for the completion of documents.

Engage in employment upon commencing a position. Having an understanding of the specific types of administrative tasks to be completed is a satisfactory initial step.

Bring the Right Identification

There exist two fundamental structures that every business should provide, namely an I-9 structure and a W-4 structure. I propose that it is imperative to consider the possibility of certain small-scale enterprises, particularly those consisting of one to five individuals, in support of my argument.

Refusing to provide you with any of them, usually the I-9 form, is a frequent occurrence. Every enterprise is expected to provide you with a W-4 form. In the event that you do not receive one, it is possible that the business might not be accurately documenting your earnings, thus giving rise to potential issues.

The I9 organizational framework is alternatively referred to as the "migration" framework. It officially attests, in writing, that you possess the privilege to pursue employment within the boundaries of the United States.

and possess the appropriate identification. There exist two distinct valid arrangements of identification that can be provided. The I9 framework requests

Potentially a singular identification or a dual identification.

Identification cards. Solely a single identification card.

If you possess a valid U.S. visa and are able to present it as a means of identification, there is no need to inconvenience yourself with additional forms of identification. If one possesses a valid green card, it is imperative to furnish said document to the employer as proof of legal authorization to work in the United States. Two IDs:

If you lack a valid visa or green card, it is imperative that you present two forms of identification. Generally speaking, an individual will assume the role of a driver.

Authorized documentation or a government-issued identification card, complete with a photograph. The alternative could encompass various documents, such as a government-issued pension card or a certified copy of a birth certificate.

Chapter Two: Securing Employment

The majority of organizations demonstrate a distinctive preference for a government-issued retirement card. It is essential to include your government-backed retirement number on the form, regardless. Moreover, it has been conveyed to organizations that they may potentially be held accountable in this regard.

Subject to the condition that your name is not verified for accuracy against the information available within your social records, you may face financial penalties. security card. By having a clear understanding of what you intend to demonstrate to your new supervisor, you are able to structure your approach accordingly. If you do not possess an authorized duplicate of your government-endorsed retirement card, please make sure to promptly request a copy. Although it is provided at no cost, it may take up to two weeks for it to be delivered to your location.

Know Your W-4

You will also be provided with another structure to complete, which is a finance structure known as

a W-4. This provides the individual with information regarding the party responsible for conducting a financial assessment, as well as the specific personal details to be reviewed, including name, address, federal retirement identification number, marital status, and preferred number of allowances to be disclosed.

Numerous individuals become perplexed regarding the appropriate entries to make on this document, typically resorting to merely marking either the "Single" or "Married" boxes and inserting a numerical value of either 1 or 0 on line 5, which pertains to deductions. That option is not necessarily unfavorable, however, there is certainly room to make more judicious decisions.

Chapter Two: Employment Acquisition

The document includes an attached worksheet designed to aid you in organizing the quantity of derivations to be placed on the structure. What you're figuring out

This refers to the calculation of the total amount of taxes and obligations levied by the government and state authorities, which will be deducted from an individual's salary during each designated period and subsequently remitted to the Internal Revenue Service (IRS). Throughout the span of a full year's worth of paychecks, the small portion of taxes withheld from each check should add up to your total tax liability (comprising of a 10% federal tax rate plus a 3% state tax rate, or a 15% federal tax rate plus a 3% state tax rate based on your gross income).

The Internal Revenue Service provides finance processors with a document outlining expense allowances, as referenced earlier in Publication 15. The "unmarried" individual has a larger amount deducted from their paycheck compared to the "married" taxpayer. Why? In a family that is united through marriage, there exists a situation where multiple individuals are dependent on the same income source. Consequently, the overall tax liability of such a family would be reduced, resulting in the IRS imposing a comparatively lower deduction from their earnings.

A "derivation" is employed to denote the number of individuals who depend on your income for their daily sustenance. Each deduction is considered as an "individual." The document acknowledges that you are eligible to claim one "derivation" for yourself and an additional one, provided that you have engaged in each occupation solely during the year. Therefore, an individual has the discretion to record either 0, 1, or 2 exclusively for their own purpose.

When selecting zero exemptions, the Internal Revenue Service (IRS) levies a greater number of assessments from that paycheck compared to opting for one or more allowances. In a similar vein, as you choose a greater number of allowances, the amount of taxes deducted from that particular income is reduced. Irrespective of whether you are the sole beneficiary of your income, you can still add additional exemptions to your W-4. The quantity of depends on your unique situation. The Internal Revenue Service does not conduct inquiries into the number of deductions ranging from 0 to 9. Exercise utmost caution in formulating your written conclusions in this context.

Consider this as a formal obligation to compile a report for your review. If we assume that you did not earn any income throughout the year and decide to pursue a different occupation, such as starting in October, it would be advisable to budget and allocate as much funds as possible from each paycheck in order to make up for the lack of previous earnings.

Payment in cash and the likelihood of minimal liabilities in terms of charges may be expected, given that you will be engaged in labor for only a period of 90 days within the fiscal year. You could possibly

Place the numerical symbol "9" onto the designated framework. In the event that you exclusively generate cash during the summer months, it is possible to consider indicating a "9" on the form.

The cost estimation for the audits conducted by the IRS is based on the annual revenue. It is permissible to appropriately increase the number of allowances on your W-4 form for a truncated fiscal year, while ensuring the maintenance of suitable measures to safeguard your financial well-being. If you have entered into employment in October, it is advisable to ensure that you modify your W-4 arrangement for the subsequent calendar year (shortly after January 1st) should you decide to retain the same position and anticipate its continuation throughout the entire year.

You have the flexibility to modify your W-4 as often as desired throughout the course of the year. That is a thoroughly valid action for you to undertake. The finance person should utilize the most recent W-4 form that you approved to complete your tax withholding.

Please verify and ensure it is retained in the records.

Certain individuals prefer to have the Internal Revenue Service alleviate a substantial amount of responsibilities from their obligations.

check. This suggests that upon recording their expenditures, individuals are guaranteed to receive a certain amount of monetary reimbursement. For individuals who struggle with saving money, this could be a beneficial arrangement, as it is highly risky to accumulate a debt with the IRS without having the funds available to fulfill the obligation. The Internal Revenue Service possesses the jurisdiction to indefinitely levy charges that you owe, eliminating any possibility of evading your obligation in the event of loan default. It stays with you. "(Insolvency is certain in Chapter 6.)

However, if you are someone who is diligent in saving, it is important to understand that any extra funds that you allow the IRS to withhold from your income throughout the course of a year will be returned to you with minimal interest. The government obtaining a short-term loan from you and returning it without compensating you for the use of your funds. If one possesses the characteristic of being a prudent saver, it is advisable to consider the option of depositing the surplus funds into a bank account, under the assumption that other factors remain consistent. By doing so, it can be ensured that when the time comes to file taxes, the funds required to remit to the IRS will already be available, and furthermore, these funds will have generated interest during the waiting period.

Therefore, in the event that we assume that you have a propensity for poor saving, it is advisable to choose the status of "Single" (even if this is not your exact marital status) and indicate "0" or "1" allowances on the relevant form, in order to avoid any potential debt owed to the IRS during the time of settlement.

To document your responsibilities and assuming you possess good saving habits, you have the option to select

Chapter 2: Securing Employment

By acquiring larger quantities of allowances, it is advisable to allocate sufficient funds to cover any additional taxes that you might be liable for, before the deadline for tax submission.

Direct Deposit

There is an additional structure that you may be requested to finalize, in the event that you

These tools are employed within a larger organization that extends assistance to you. If you submit a voided check (ensuring that you mark it clearly with the word VOID) to your employer and provide your authorized signature, your payroll department will be able to initiate direct deposit of your salary into your designated bank account. There should be a continuous flow of movement, and individuals should refrain from lingering in queues.

This assistance should not incur any costs for you; however, it is imperative that you make a decision to grant your employer access to your personal financial records. If you appreciate this assistance, please ensure that you bring at least one voided check to be supplied to or duplicated by the finance office. Should you desire to maintain the integrity of your data and prioritize your security, it would be inappropriate for your manager to compel your participation. Nevertheless, there exist a limited number of organizations that primarily remunerate their employees in this manner, and they may insist on it.

The Intersections Of The Economy And The Financial Markets

Although the economy and the financial markets are distinct entities, they exert influence upon each other. The capital obtained through market investment is allocated towards the development and expansion of enterprises, thereby generating employment opportunities for individuals who can subsequently purchase goods and services produced by these firms. This process not only stimulates economic growth but also yields profits for shareholders.

What is the definition of Economics?

Adam Smith, a distinguished Scottish philosopher of the 18th century, is widely acknowledged as the progenitor of contemporary economics. Smith gained widespread recognition for his seminal work, "The Wealth of Nations," published in 1776. A renowned British economist of his time, Alfred Marshall presented a formal definition of economics as the systematic examination of human behavior in mundane business affairs.

Economics encompasses virtually all facets of human existence. The economy may be perceived as a transfer or exchange of commodities and services amid producers and consumers. The movement of goods and services occurs unilaterally, whereas the movement of income and expenditure occurs reciprocally.

Economics is a discipline rooted in the study of society, focused on the intricate dynamics of producing, allocating, and utilizing goods and services. It examines how individuals, businesses, governments, and nations make decisions regarding the efficient allocation of limited resources. Scarcity refers to the condition wherein the demands of individuals for goods, services, and resources surpass the available supply. The primary objective of economics is to enhance the quality of life for individuals in their routine existence. Due to the inherent limitations of resources, it is imperative for societies to establish clear priorities and make thoughtful decisions regarding the optimal allocation of resources to fulfill a wide range of needs and desires to the greatest extent possible.

Fundamentally, economics endeavors to elucidate the rationale behind our decision-making processes when it comes to purchasing goods and services. Several fundamental economic principles, namely scarcity, supply and demand, costs and benefits, and incentives, can elucidate a multitude of decisions made by individuals.

Economics can also furnish invaluable insights for making decisions in various aspects of daily living. From an individual standpoint, economics plays a fundamental role in shaping numerous decisions that we are obliged to make concerning employment, recreation, consumption, and the extent of our savings. The trajectory of our lives is also impacted by macroeconomic factors, encompassing phenomena such as inflation, prevailing interest rates, and overall economic expansion.

The findings of a newly conducted research conducted by the International Labour Office (ILO) shed light on the fact that individuals' financial stability plays a crucial role in fostering personal welfare, contentment, and inclusiveness, thereby facilitating progress and advancement.

One illustration of economics could be the analysis of the stock market. Economics pertains to the systematic examination of wealth production, distribution, and consumption, encompassing a range of interconnected concerns such as labor, finance, taxation, among others.

What is the correlation between the stock markets and the economy?

The capital market assumes a vital role in fostering the expansion of commerce and industry, thereby exerting a consequential impact on the overall economic landscape of the nation. That is why the industrial entities, governmental consultants, and even the national monetary authority closely monitor the operations of the stock market. One can achieve economic growth by augmenting the scale of the stock markets within a nation, along with enhancing the market capitalization in an emerging market such as South Africa.

Multiple research studies in the field of economics have consistently demonstrated a direct correlation between the expansion of the economy and the advancement of the stock market. A meticulously structured and effectively governed stock market generates investment prospects within the nation through the provision of funding for productive ventures that contribute to economic vitality, optimizes the allocation of capital, mobilizes domestic savings, contributes to risk diversification, and facilitates the exchange of goods and services.

Furthermore, the stock market assumes a pivotal function in appropriating capital to the corporate sphere, thereby exerting a tangible impact on overall economic growth.

Fluctuations in stock markets are frequently influenced by macroeconomic indicators such as interest rates, inflation, unemployment rates, and economic growth. The stock markets consistently advocate for increased economic growth as it generally leads to enhanced profitability for businesses and subsequently fosters appreciation in the value of stocks traded on the financial markets.

What are the primary classifications that define the economy?

The discipline of economics is characterized by its division into two distinct components, specifically. macroeconomics and microeconomics. Macroeconomics pertains to the entirety of the economy, encompassing its complete scope. The objective is to gain comprehension of the functioning of the overall economy in relation to factors such as economic growth, price stability, full employment, and balance of payments stability. It is sought to ascertain which policy measures have the potential to enhance the economy's performance.

Macroeconomics aims to elucidate the factors behind disparities in economic growth rates between nations, fluctuations in annual inflation rates, elevated levels of unemployment, the relative weakness of certain currencies like the rand vis-à-vis robust currencies such as the US dollar, and occasional rapid surges in imports of goods and services.

Microeconomics places its emphasis on the individual units of decision-making and their interplay with each other. This examines the actions of individuals, households, businesses, government, and the foreign sector and analyzes the consequences derived from their conduct. A considerable portion of the field of microeconomics revolves around undertaking market analyses.

Who are the principal actors in the economy?

Producers engage in the exchange of goods and services with consumers. Consequently, it is incumbent upon consumers to remunerate for the goods and services they have acquired. These individuals generate income through the exchange of their labor in return for salaries and wages. A portion of domestic production is directed towards foreign markets, while additional goods and services are imported to meet the needs of the domestic market.

What are the determinants of economic growth?

Economic growth is solely the result of augmenting the calibre and quantity of the components of production, encompassing four overarching categories: land, labor, capital, and entrepreneurship.

What are the primary components that constitute an economy?

National accounts quantify the circulation of commodities, services, and monetary assets. They serve as the paramount means of obtaining information regarding the conditions and dynamics of the economy. The national accounts comprise indicators such as Gross Domestic Product (GDP), gross domestic expenditure, and gross national income.

The Gross Domestic Product (GDP) serves as an indicator of the comprehensive economic activity transpiring within a given economy. This includes the entirety of goods and services generated within the economy during a specific timeframe. In the context of South Africa, the Gross Domestic Product is assessed both on a quarterly and an annual basis. Gross Domestic Product (GDP) is quantified based on prevailing market prices. This represents the official calculation of the nation's Gross Domestic Product.

Investors demonstrate a heightened interest in real GDP, which accounts for the influence of inflation. This is accomplished by assessing the gross domestic product (GDP) while keeping prices constant. The Gross Domestic Product (GDP) represents a fundamental and significant gauge or benchmark for assessing the economic performance. This encompasses private consumption, which refers to the expenditure made by private households on consumer goods, alongside government consumption expenditure at the national, provincial, and local levels.

Gross National Income (GNI) or Gross National Product (GNP) refers to the comprehensive monetary worth of all income garnered by the individuals who hold citizenship or permanent residency within a particular nation. This provision pertains to the exclusion of all earnings generated by foreign individuals and foreign-owned enterprises, while encompassing earnings accrued by South African citizens residing overseas.

The Balance of Payments serves as a comprehensive account detailing all commercial exchanges undertaken between the inhabitants of a nation and foreign entities over a designated timeframe. This encompasses a wide spectrum of actors, ranging from individuals, corporations, and governmental bodies, facilitating the transfer of tangible commodities, services, resources, presents, and all monetary dealings.

The fundamental pillars of a market-based economy are hinged upon the principles of supply and demand. Supply pertains to the quantity of goods or services that the market is capable of providing at a particular price. Demand pertains to the extent of the desired quantity of a particular product or service by purchasers at this specific price. As the price of goods or services increases, the demand for them decreases, and conversely, as the price decreases, the demand increases. When the quantities demanded and supplied are balanced, it is deemed that the economy has attained a state of equilibrium.

Fiscal and Monetary Policy. Authorities impose taxes in order to fund their expenditures. They must thus make decisions regarding the allocation of funds, the choice of expenditures, and the methods of financing these outlays. This is referred to as fiscal policy. The primary tool of fiscal policy is the Budget, which is submitted to Parliament on a yearly basis by the Minister of Finance during the month of February. The Minister expounds upon the Government's financial allocation proposals for the fiscal year, which spans from 01 April to 31 March of the subsequent year, during the Budget Speech. The Minister also outlines the proposed funding sources for the expenditure, such as taxation, loans, and other relevant means.

Monetary policy encompasses the range of actions undertaken by the South African Reserve Bank (SARB) to impact the supply of money or the interest rate, with the purpose of attaining price stability, promoting higher employment rates, and fostering economic expansion.

www.ingramcontent.com/pod-product-compliance
Lightning Source LLC
Chambersburg PA
CBHW071646210326
41597CB00017B/2132